Sons Love Drawing Mutant Robot Battles With Dads

Valentin Martinez & Aaron Ross

Sons Love Drawing Mutant Robot Battles With Dads

ISBN: 978-0-9843802-2-0

PebbleStorm, Inc.
8605 Santa Monica Blvd, #39743
West Hollywood, CA 90069

Contact: info@pebblestorm.com

www.UniqueGenius.com
www.PebbleStorm.com
www.CEOFlow.com

Limits of Liability and Disclaimer of Warranty

Warning - Disclaimer

This book is dedicated to:

…Valentin, an incredible boy, son and Transformer fighter!

…and to Mom, Aurora and Pari, the wonderful women of the Ross family who show so much love and patience with us :)

Welcome!

Hi guys,

Ever had those times when it's a rainy day, a weekend or you just aren't sure what you want to do, or what you want to play?

Well, drawing mutant robot battles together is both fun and a great bonding activity!

We have written a simple book on how to have fun and drawing these battles. It is especially fun playing together.

We have advice for both kids and dads in this book.

Have fun playing!

Aaron ("Air"– age 39) & Valentin ("Bud"– age 6)

What You Need

To draw mutant battles, you need:

1) Two blank pieces of paper – one for each of you.

2) Two black pens, crayons or pencils – so you can both draw at the same time.

3) A space to put the paper and draw where you won't mess up furniture or get in anyone's way (like mom).

That's it!

PS - You don't need anything more than black... but yellow, orange and red crayons are perfect for rocket engine flames, lasers and explosions, or stars in outer space.

Also, blue, brown and green pens or crayons helps with coloring water, earth and space worlds.

Closeup!

How To Draw Battles (Instructions)

We have sample pictures for you to copy, but you can create anything you want. In fact, instead of robots, you could draw bugs, Transformers, Pokemon, monsters or any thing else that battles.

Here are some suggestions:

1. Copy our pictures or make up your own.

2. Help your dad draw – he may not know what the best robots or monsters are, or how to draw them.

3. You can always add more missiles, claws, guns or lasers to anything you draw.

4. Don't make it look too nice, drawing them mEsSY is part of the fun. This isn't an art contest.

5. When you draw an explosion, make sure you yell "BOOM!!" while you draw it - that's the most fun part.

6. Have fun and be as silly or crazy as you want...

Now put this down and go draw your first robot!!

This battle included an underground fortress with ships and a robot fighting:

Battles Can Be As Big As You Want Over Lots Of Pages

Battles can take place on the ground. Or in the air. Or under ground. Or in space.

You could also draw them in crazy places like the inside of our Sun, in a mudpit, or inside an office building, or your kitchen, or any place else you want.

You can have them go as high as you want in to the air or space! Or as deep into the ocean or earth as you want.

Add as many pages as you want to your battle, in any direction. We like to tape them together into big worlds that go from underground to outer space.

A big world battle we drew while on vacation:

Left: Valentin in his PJs; Right: mom Jessica helping hold it up.

While Drawing, Say "BOOM" With Explosions & Make Star Wars Laser Sounds

When you draw explosions, the best part is actually saying "BOOM!" when you draw it.

Dads – you have to say it too!

In fact, the more sounds you make while drawing, the better.

When a robot or space ship shoots a laser, make Star Wars laser sounds ("P-CHEWP-CHEWP-CHEW") while you draw the laser shots, and then when the laser hits something, yell your "KA-BOOM!"

You too dad!

A good guy ship shooting a
robot with a laser:

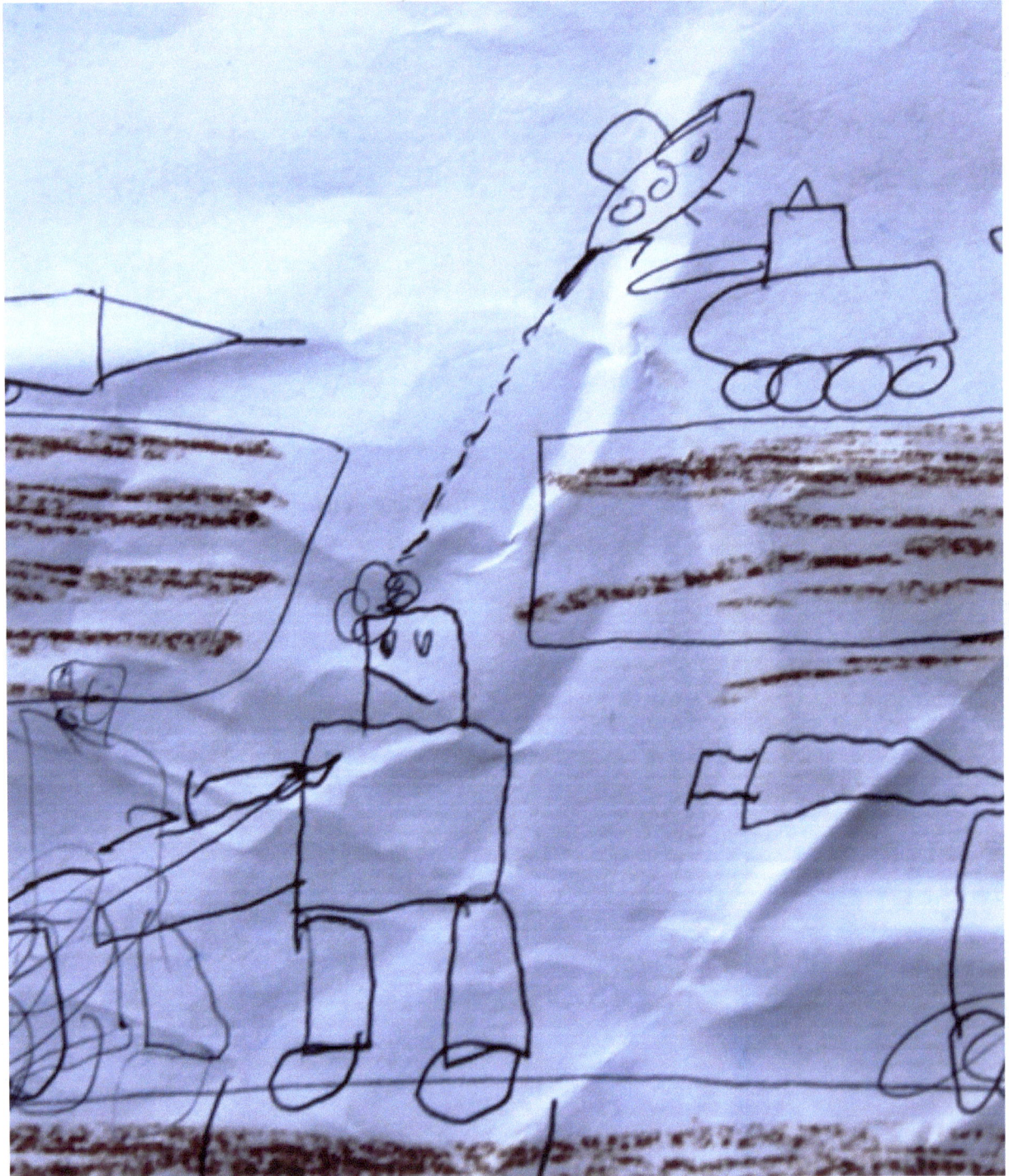

No Electronics Or Email When Playing

Sometimes dads leave electronics and phones on when they should be off (like when drawing with you or at meals).

Remind him no checking email while playing.

Also, you need to turn the television off too. No internet or TV allowed while you play.

You can play music while you draw.

Any one can also call "Time Out" while drawing if you need to take a break to do something, like eat or go to the bathroom or clean up.

Remember to call "Time In" when you're done, so every-one knows when to start again.

Drawing space battles needs focus. No email, television or internet while playng!

When You Get Frustrated, ARGH!!

Sometimes when you draw you might get frustrated, or it stops being fun.

For example, when you want to draw an awesome alien spaceship but you just can't get it right. Argh!!

If that happens, take what ever you are drawing and blow it up with some HUGE explosions and yell "KA-BOOM KA-BOOM KA-BOOM" alot!!!

If you get EXTRA upset or really frustrated, break some pencils too!!

Valentin drew some BOOMs here for fun:

Help Dad To Have Fun & Play

Some dads have forgotten how to play.

Because they can work a lot to care for your family, sometimes it has been a long time since a dad has played. He might have forgotten how. The good news is any dad can learn to have fun again.

You can help remind him how to have fun by showing him what you like to do.

If your dad isn't having fun remind him: "Dad, you are supposed to be drawing, so draw. Draw a missile exploding an alien and yell BOOM!"

Or ask him to take a break for a pillow fight or wrestling!

What other ways can you help dad have fun?

Air had lots of fun drawing this submarine in a lake,with an underwater passage to a secret base

Tell A Story While You Draw

While you draw your aliens, mutants or robots, is there a story here?

Is there a mega-robot fighting against all the aliens? Or are there mutants fighting transformers?

What are the bosses trying to conquer?

"This mega boss wants to capture your underground fortress. Now he is shooting a missile bomb at your gate to destroy it ("BOOM!!") so his small guys can invade and capture it..."

Tell the story while you draw!

In this 4-page battle, a mega-robot was so powerful it took two pages to hold it. It was so tall it stood on the ground and its head was in space.

Dads Might Need Help Drawing Messy

If your dad keeps trying to show you how to draw a ship better, that is nice of him. But making ships look good does not make them more fun or powerful.

Lots of dads have something called "perfectionism". It means they don't want to draw anything unless it looks really nice. BORING!!!

You might need to help him learn how to draw messier which is more fun!

Remember:

- Messy is best-y

- Just draw it!

- Don't worry, be crappy

- Being meticulous is ridiculous!

First Valentin drew a small tank, then Air knew how to draw a big tank like it.

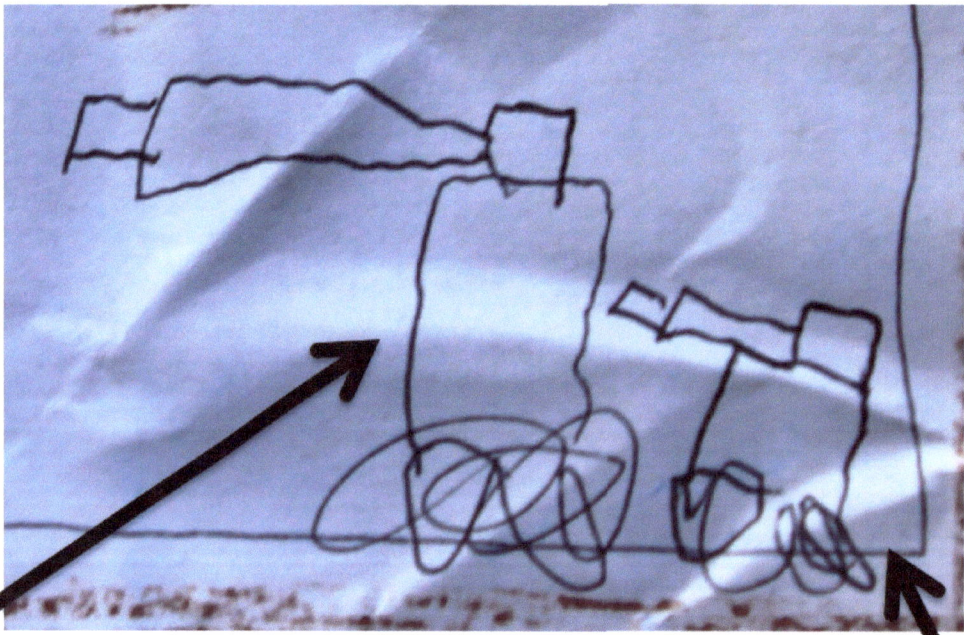

Air's Tank

Valentin's Tank

Go Crazy!

Have a great time drawing battles...

You can't make them too messy. They do not need to look good or pretty (that's for girls).

Here was an awesome one! Notice there were lots of robots, ships and explosions.

Just For Dads

I hope you have a great time with your son drawing battles!

It's really important to understand that YOU are getting and learning as much from this as your son is, including:

• PATIENCE – you might have to work on a battle a few minutes a time over weeks. When your son wants to do it, go for it! When he doesn't, don't push it. Put out the tools, but let him come to you.

• IMPERFECTIONISM - Learn how to let go of looking good, and be messy - copy your son's drawings style... draw like them. Don't try to get them to draw like you.

• ENCOURAGEMENT - not criticism – if you catch yourself thinking any negative thoughts about your son's drawing, his impatience, his ADD, quality of story, etc... shut yer trap. Only encouragement and positive belief in your son, not criticism.

• SHOW, DON'T TELL – don't tell him what to do or be, show him by being a great role model. No matter what you say, kids copy what you do. Any attitude of "do as I say, not as I do" is harmful to your relationship with him.

• MAKE SOUNDS - lots of them while you draw – BOOMs, KA-BOOMs, laser sounds, anything. It makes it much more interactive and fun. You could even take it to the next level and act it out!

• CREATIVITY - we've given you a starting point, take it and do whatever you want to make it work for your family, including daughters or older sons.

• LET GO and let yourself have some fun! If it's hard at first, keep at it. You can relearn how.

Air & Valentin

2011

Blank Space To Draw Battles
Your First Battle Book

Blank Space To Draw Battles
Your First Battle Book

Blank Space To Draw Battles
Your First Battle Book

Blank Space To Draw Battles
Your First Battle Book

www.ingramcontent.com/pod-product-compliance
Lightning Source LLC
Chambersburg PA
CBHW042002100426
42813CB00019B/2954